MOMENTS

POEMS OF
LIFE AND LOVE

KATHRYN CAROLE ELLISON

Published by Lady Bug Books, an imprint of Brisance Books Group.
Lady Bug Press and the distinctive ladybug logo are registered trademarks of
Lady Bug Books, LLC.

Lady Bug Books
400 112th Avenue N.E.
Suite 230
Bellevue, WA 98004
www.GiftsOfLove.com

For information about custom editions, special sales and permissions, please email
Info@GiftsOfLove.com

Manufactured in the United States of America
ISBN: 978-1-944194-68-0

First Edition: November 2020

A NOTE FROM THE AUTHOR

The poems in this book were written over many years as gifts to my children. I began writing them in the 1970s, when they were reaching the age of reason. And, as I found myself in the position of becoming a single parent, I wanted to do something special to share with them—something that would become a tradition, a ritual they could count on.

And so the Advent Poems began—one day, decades ago—with a poem 'gifted' to them each day during the Advent period leading up to Christmas, December 1 to December 24. Forty some years later... my children still look forward each year to the poems that started a family tradition, that new generations have come to cherish.

It is my sincere hope that you will embrace and enjoy them, and share them with those you love.

Children of the Light was among the early poems I wrote, and is included in each of the *Poems of Life and Love* books in The Ellison Collection: *Heartstrings, Celebrations, Inspirations, Sanctuary, Awakenings, Sojourns, Milestones, Tapestry, Gratitude, Beginnings, Horizons* and *Moments*. After writing many hundreds of poems, it is still my favorite. The words came from my heart... and my soul... and flowed so effortlessly that it was written in a single sitting.
All I needed to do was capture the words on paper.

Light, to me, represented all that was good and pure and right with the world, and I believed then—as I do today—that those elements live in my children, and perhaps in all of us. We need only to dare.

– KCE

DEDICATION

To my parents: Herb and Bernice Haas

Mom, you were the poet who went before me...
unpublished, but appreciated nonetheless.

And Dad, you always believed in me,
no matter what direction my life took.
Thank you for your faith in me,
and for your unconditional love.

TABLE OF CONTENTS

LIFE'S JOYS

LIFE'S LESSONS

LIFE'S GIFTS

LIFE'S JOYS

SURRENDER

Always say "yes" to the present moment.
It's futile to resist what already is.
It would be insane to oppose life itself,
Which is now, it's now. Now it is!

Surrender to what is; say "yes" to life,
And be amazed at the results that come next.
Life suddenly starts working for, not against, you.
Let the world embrace you, don't be perplexed.

Amazing things happen when you surrender and just love;
You melt into the power already within you.
The world changes when you change, and softens when you soften.
The world loves you when you decide to love it, too.

Be willing to let go of the life that you have,
So you can have the life that is waiting in the wings.
If you surrender completely to each present moment,
You'll live more richly as human beings.

MUSIC

Music is to the soul what words are to the mind.
It's the universal language of mankind.
It can name the unnameable and communicate the unknowable.
It exists to speak the words we cannot find.

Music is a world within itself
With a language we all understand.
Music calms one's soul, takes one to another place,
Away from the problems at hand.

Nietzsche proclaimed that life would be a mistake
Without music. It expresses the inexpressible.
Jack Kerouac wrote, "The only truth is music."
It's everywhere and, thankfully, accessible.

Music clears your head and heals your heart.
It's a lifter of spirits; it brings joy.
It's a form of communication; it's a way to show emotion
With the soothing sounds of music you enjoy.

CHILDREN OF THE LIGHT

There are those souls who bring the light,
Who spill it out for all to share.
And with a joy that does excite,
They show the world that they do care.
It is so very bright.

In this sharing, love does pervade
Into their lives and cycles round;
And as this light is outward played
The love is also inward bound.
It is an awesome trade.

You are a soul whose light is shared.
It comes from deep within your heart.
It's best because it is not spared,
Because it's total, not just part.
And I am glad you've dared.

HESITATION

"He who hesitates is lost!"
An expression attributed to the actress, Mae West.
(In case some of you don't know who she was,
Then "google" her name; she lived life to the fullest!)

Hesitation, or doubt, can kill more dreams
Than failure, or even hardship, ever could.
It's your fear that causes your hesitation.
Courage will bring success, in all likelihood.

Hesitation enlarges, or magnifies, your fear.
By taking action promptly, and being decisive,
The flutters in your heart will vanish; yes, they will.
Then success, for you, will not be elusive.

Move forward in your lives, with no second guessing.
That means no "guilt trips," and no hesitation.
Re-creating yourself anew each moment,
Without fear, requires your full participation.

STILLNESS

Most of us treat the present moment as an obstacle
To overcome in order to reach a far-away goal.
(But the present moment – now – is Life, itself.)
It's an insane way to live, and takes a toll.

Slow down, enjoy life, and pause for a view,
Or nothing worthwhile will catch up to you.
You'll not only miss the scenery as it whizzes by –
You'll lose the sense of where you're going, and why.

Learn to become still, and your wisdom will come.
Stillness cures all the sickness of the soul.
Just look and listen. No more is needed.
Carry your stillness with you. It is your role.

Being still does not mean "don't move" at all.
It means "Move in Peace" from morning to nightfall.
And in the midst of chaos and confusion/disarray,
Keep stillness inside of you, it's a known pathway.

Learn how to be still, to really be still,
And let life happen, to know who you are.
Your stillness becomes a radiance you emit.
Adopt the patient pace of nature and go far.

Wherever you go in the midst of movement and activity,
Carry your stillness with you. Carry it with dignity.
It will keep open your access to your creativity,
Which for you is your field of pure potentiality.

You must know stillness before you can learn your true song.
Stillness is a sanctuary to which you can retreat.
A great silent space holds all of nature in its embrace.
It also holds you. Yourself you will meet.

SLOW DOWN

"There is more to life than increasing its speed."
(Gandhi is credited with these very wise words.)
It's great advice for simplifying your life.
The benefits from slowing down should not be ignored.

First start with yourself; slow down your breathing.
Become aware of each in– and ex–halation.
When driving, slow down and become more aware
Of where you are, with less agitation.

Slow down your speech and your inner thoughts.
Slow down the frantic pace of everything you do.
Take time to hear others; I mean, really listen.
Check your inclination to interrupt; Let their truth come through.

Stop to enjoy the stars shining bright,
And notice the cloud formations on a semi–clear day.
Rejoin the perfect pace at which creation works.
Join the perfection of nature's plan today.

Inside information

You are the only one who knows what's best for you.
Your life is filled with tasks that only you can do.
You are the only one who knows your own life's plan.
You choose your path; you are the only one who can.

All choices start at sources found inside your heart.
Because of first-hand knowledge you can play your part
And know that all the choices that exist for you
Are yours to think and play with as you'll often do.

Take heart, my loves, because with knowledge there is power.
Knowing yourself can make your strength a tower.
From what you know of your life map – its every line –
Please know you will make choices that for you are fine.

LEAVE A LEGACY TIME CAN'T ERASE

If your name is carved on hearts
And not on tombstones when you die,
Your legacy will be etched into the minds of others.
The stories will be shared; they'll multiply.

Your goal is not to live forever;
It's to be creative with something that will.
You make your mark by being true to yourself.
Your decisions and actions emit good will.

As Maya Angelou shared in some of her writings:
"People will forget what you said (no appeal).
They'll also forget what you did, my friends,
But they will never forget how you made them feel."

The legacy you leave is the life you lead.
(It may be time to take an inventory.)
The people you see, the decisions you make,
And the actions you take... that's your story.

Remember, you're in charge of what you leave behind.
Take control of your life, no limits to perceive.
Society cannot tell you how it's going to be.
You get to decide the legacy that you will leave.

PERFECTION

God does not send us pain, my friends,
Nor damnation to our souls.
We do it to ourselves – you know,
And pay our various tolls.

It's said that the obstacles we throw up
Will aid us on our path –
The path to perfection of our souls
Which will come in the aftermath.

Those having many trials in their lives
Are perfecting faster by their own choice,
But taking it fast or taking it slow –
The end's the same. We rejoice!!

We will all arrive at the lovely point –
The point of self-contentment;
And remain forever on the other side
Where troubles are non-existent.

Life happens

Events are impersonal – they happen, that's that.
How we regard them, or read them, tells volumes about us!
Undisciplined people, driven by their hostilities and regrets
Look for signs that reinforce their own unexamined views.

Wiser people, however, watch for how they can respond,
Extract a lesson, apply it later when something similar occurs.
It takes courage to search for the hidden lesson
Because others will react with judgment, you can be sure.

These simplistic responses can obscure the more creative
Ways to look at an event when it transpires.
And the wise person knows that projecting the worst
Based on childish hopes and fears will always backfire.

When considering the future remember this truth:
Situations unfold as they do, notwithstanding.
How we feel about them – our judgment –
Our hopes and our fears sway our understanding.

BEAUTY

In every person's heart there is a secret nerve
That answers to the vibrations of beauty.
Let the beauty of what you love be what you do.
For true happiness, it becomes your duty.

If the path is beautiful don't ask where it leads.
You will be guided to a better location.
Beauty is the promise of happiness.
Take the path without hesitation.

Love of beauty is one of Nature's best healers.
Our souls need beauty more than food.
What a man does for pay is nothing when compared
To his response to beauty, when viewed.

Joy in looking and comprehending
Is Nature's most beautiful gift.
Let us live for the beauty of our own reality,
And watch our spirits lift.

If you keep the ability to always see beauty,
Your spirit will never grow old.
Beauty is power, a smile is its sword.
It's a way of life that's age-old.

INSPIRATIONAL lifE

Albert Einstein had a very bright mind.
He was remembered for his formula, E=mc squared.
But he is also known for some very wise words.
Regarding inspiration, these words he shared:
"There are two ways to live your life," said he,
"One is as though nothing is a miracle;
The other is as though everything is."
Was Einstein some kind of oracle?

In doing, don't ask what the world needs.
Ask only what makes you come alive.
Then go do it, and make the world a better place.
It needs more people who thrive!

And don't worry about failures; no, not a bit.
Sure, you might end up having some of them.
Worry instead about the chances you'd miss;
When you don't even try, it's a problem.

You alone must build your very own dreams
For a life of happiness, you know;
Or someone will hire you to build some for them,
Leaving you to live a life of sorrow.

CONTENTMENT

Alfred Nobel, in his wisdom, after thinking it through,
Declared that contentment is the only real wealth.
Faithfulness has been described as the best relationship,
And the wisest all agree that the greatest gift is health.

So, now, how to achieve it? This feeling of contentment?
We begin, my friends, with a grateful heart.
It's the foundation for the development of many virtues.
Contentment is one, I wish to impart.

Good humor is a tonic for mind and body.
It's an antidote for anxiety and depression.
It attracts and keeps friends, it lightens human burdens.
It's a direct route to contentment, a loving expression.

SHORTCOMINGS

As you learn to see others' shortcomings with wit
You'll be able to face your own.
And work to change and improve and grow...
And for hurts you've given, atone.

Remember this, it's your mind that makes
Your faults so big or so small.
Your imagination can create a monster size
Or one that's not very big at all.

Good humor helps when you work on you.
It makes the work much easier, by far.
It helps you see for yourself just how
Wonderful you really are!

PATIENCE

A little test for you to take
To determine your patience level
Is to check the speedometer on your car
As you drive down the street pell mell.

If you slow down and take more time,
Hear your friends' stories, increase your 'smarts,'
(Believe me, I know from experience...) you are
Less likely to break things, even hearts.

LIFE'S LESSONS

LOVERS AND HATERS

Hate is as all absorbing as love is, any day.
It's as irrational as love, and in its own way
It can be an oddly fulfilling and satisfying display.

Lovers see each other, and do a handspring.
Haters dream of meeting their objects 'in the ring,'
And revel in thoughts of them sprawling and hurting.

The major difference between loving and hating
Is not the heart beat that is loud and pulsating,
Nor the adrenaline flow that is most fascinating.

Loving fulfills, enriches, and is freeing,
While hating compromises one's well-being.
(The differences a blind man could be seeing!)

The lover simply loves; so easily, unassuming –
The hater is best when he's fussing and fuming.
The passion of the hater is ultimately self-consuming.

FEAR OF DARKNESS, FEAR OF LIGHT (IT'S ALL JUST FEAR)

When children are young, sometimes they are
Afraid of the dark and what might be
There to frighten them out of their wits.
You've seen it. I'm sure you'll agree.

Fortunately, most of them outgrow those fears
As they mature and experience more of life.
They keep learning new things about their world –
Sometimes, with a great deal of strife.

Nevertheless, they learn and they grow,
And make their way down life's highway.
And dark turns to light with each new challenge;
Knowledge becomes the norm of the day.

But sometimes, the fear does not go away;
It stays, but in a different form.
The dark becomes comfortable, or safer, somehow
Than stepping up to transform.

Some people avoid growing or changing
With all their power and might.
The tragedy, my friends, is when grown men
Are deathly afraid of the light.

PROGRESS

Perhaps the word "progress" can mean one thing to you,
And another thing to them, or to me.
But we come to full agreement on the fact
That progress always requires change, you see.

George Bernard Shaw weighed in on the subject:
"Progress is impossible without change."
He added that people who could not change their minds
Could not change anything. (Not so strange)

Thomas Edison said that "... discontent
Is the first necessity of progress."
And Mahatma Gandhi added "healthy" in front of
The word "discontent," but I digress.

The world hates change, or so it seems,
But progress is, without it, a nonentity.
In fact, I've heard it said quite often
That change is the only inevitability.

Progress in life comes not through adaptation,
But through daring, stepping into the unknown.
Think of the turtle who makes progress only
When he sticks his neck out (of his safety zone).

HOLDING A GRUDGE

Holding a grudge may feel good for a while.
You've been hurt... unnecessarily so.
The other person took advantage or wronged you somehow,
And the pain is too delicious to let go.

You relive the experience, mulling it over and over.
As the momentum increases, you seethe with indignation.
You might tell other people how you were wronged,
And to justify the anger, you get confirmation.

Confucius once said that being wronged is nothing
Unless you continue to remember the pain.
Negative feelings (grudges) will swallow you up.
Release them with forgiveness, don't live them over again.

Holding a grudge is like holding a hand grenade...
It will destroy you if you don't let it go.
Life is too short to waste your days
Dwelling on what happened a long time ago.

Forgive others... not because they ˙deserve˙ your forgiveness,
But because you owe yourself peace.
The anger you hold inside hurts only you.
Let go, forgive, you'll enjoy the release.

Another way to look at forgiving the wrong
(As if, by now, you need another nudge):
Let your hands be so busy catching your blessings
That you don't have the capacity to hold on to a grudge.

BE STILL

Watch the rain – it always stops.
And that's true for thunder as well.
No natural outpouring goes on and on,
So speak briefly if you've something to tell.
A leader teaches more through being than
Through doing; his glibness to quell.
The quality of one's silence tells more, by far,
Than the casting of one's verbal spell.

Be still and follow your inner wisdom.
To know it you have to be still.
Your words carry weight when they're deeply felt;
They also carry good will.
When leading others, sincerity counts;
It guarantees effective skill.
When you're in touch with your own true Source
You consciously cooperate at will.

When you work hand in hand with your Source
Your effectiveness has great appeal;
But if you are only playing a game,
Your motives you can't conceal.
Remember that the method is
An awareness-of-process deal.
Reflect. Be still. Be true to yourself.
What do you deeply feel?

TAKE TIME FOR YOUR HEALTH

Everyone I have known who has lived a long life
(And many other dear friends who haven't)
Has said to me, "If you have your health,
You have it all!" (Message is consistent.)

The number one health problem in the world today
Seems to be based on problems of obesity.
How can one possibly live a spiritual life
If gorging on food is one's propensity?

Remember, your stomach is the size of a fist,
Not some enormous cavity needing to be filled.
By exercising your bodies... even taking a walk...
Your dreams of better health will be fulfilled.

DIGNITY

Nobility of bearing... elevation of character...
True dignity cannot be pretended... ever!
It's a quality that is hardest of all to acquire;
But, with steadfastness, can be yours forever.

Dignity is not negotiable, either.
It's the honor of the family of which you're a part.
Along with dignity you possess self-respect.
(These words of wisdom come straight from my heart.)

The ideal person bears the accidents of life
With dignity and grace his life through.
She makes the best of the circumstances.
Dignity carries, in life, a very high value.

Maturity is the ability to think, speak and act
Your feelings within the bounds of dignity.
The measure of your maturity is how spiritual you become.
In the midst of your frustrations do you show integrity?

GENEROSITY

True generosity is an offering.
It is given freely, no strings.
There are no expectations attached.
It is given with your blessings.

There's evidence that treating others
With generosity and respect
Is likely to be more natural
(And have a longer lasting effect)
If you have a higher level
Of genuine self-respect.

Generosity and gentleness
Are qualities that show no favor
To any one organized religion
Or any specific sponsor.
No, generosity is person to person.
It is kindness in every endeavor.

FREEDOM IS AN INSIDE JOB

You must first know it is an inside job
To really know what it means to be free
(And from yourself you cannot ever flee).
Fear is the culprit that from you will rob
Your faith and trust and confidence, you see.
I think you know this and that you agree.

Exhilaration comes in giving up
The habit of attachment to the old,
And dancing fearlessly, free of its hold.
You then replace the stuff in that old cup
With faith in your ability to mold
Your lives in paths both sensitive and bold.

The trust that you have in your own good works,
And in the knowledge that God's help is there,
Will give you all the confidence to dare.
No one with inner freedom ever shirks
Tasks that appear to be too much to bear.
So shake those fears and thrive beyond compare.

HONESTY

"Being honest may not get you a lot of friends,
But you can be sure it will get you the right ones."
John Lennon shared that wisdom; he left a legacy.
These days honesty is not everyone's companion.

Tell a lie once and all your truths
Become questionable. You can't be trusted.
Though honesty and transparency make you vulnerable,
Be honest and transparent... well adjusted.

Honesty is a very expensive gift,
So don't expect it from people who are "cheap."
Though honesty always saves everyone's time,
Trusting cheap people can cause you to weep.

The things you do when no one is looking
Are the things which define who you are.
You prove your integrity day by day
By keeping promises... truth will take you far!

There are four very important words in life:
Love, Honesty, Truth and Respect.
Without these in your life, you have nothing at all.
So, tell the truth! True friends you will collect.

QUESTIONS

What about him, and what about her?
Should I move here or go there, or what?
The questions you ask – the confusion that results,
Seems impossible for you to unknot.

The ten thousand questions that plague your mind
Are really one question, do you hear?
If you cut through to that one question, the core,
The ten thousand questions disappear.

Cutting through your noise to find the answer
Can be troublesome. You hit the brick wall.
But it's worth the work. The goal is golden.
With your answer, you have it all.

If questions persist, and they probably will,
Console yourself. You're not alone.
All questioning is a way of avoiding going deep.
Just know your answer is already known.

ACT WELL THE ROLE YOU HAVE BEEN GIVEN

What role in life have you selected for yourself?
And in what style are you going to play it?
Divine Will has a hand in assigning our role,
But choices we make can weight it.

Some of us will act in only a short drama;
And for some, the performance will be long...
The roles we accept must be played to perfection.
If it's difficult, remember, complaining is wrong.

Wherever you find yourself in your life's role
Give an impeccable performance. Do your best!
Whatever your role, play it with all your might.
Enjoy your life! In yourself, invest!

HUMOR

It's said that laughter is an instant vacation.
It's the best antidote for anxiety and depression.
There's more logic in humor than in anything else.
It leaves on your face an attractive expression.

Humor may not be everyone's cup of tea,
But all in all, it is mankind's greatest blessing.
Situations in your life may not be able to be changed,
But humor can change your attitude, I am guessing.

Joy in one's heart and laughter on one's lips
Is a sign that the person has a good grasp of things.
Humor is the affectionate communication of insight.
It allows one to experience many happy endings.

Some say comedy is a fun way of being serious.
It's the most significant activity of the human brain.
Humor's the direct route to serenity and contentment.
It's a state of being we all wish to obtain.

Start every day off with a smile on your lips.
(There's no visible proof there's joy in the hereafter.)
Humor's one of the best ingredients of survival.
The most wasted of days is one without laughter.

BE AN ORIGINAL

Be Original! Be Yourself! Be like no one else!
(I know... you've heard these words before.)
Be a voice, not the echo in an echo chamber.
Be not afraid of being bold, I implore!

Be who you are! Hold nothing back.
Don't be a second-rate impersonation.
It is better to fail in originality.
Yes, better, than to succeed in imitation.

You are the one thing in life that you can control.
You're an original you! Be not mistaken.
As Oscar Wilde so aptly put in words,
"Be yourself! Everybody else is already taken!"

LIFE'S GIFTS

SIMPLICITY

In character, in manner, in style... in all things...
The supreme excellence is simplicity.
Elegance is achieved when all that is superfluous
Gets discarded, leaving authenticity.

Truth is found in simplicity, and not
In multiplicity and confusion.
Simplicity is the key to avoiding complication.
Needing an abundance of things is an illusion.

Lao Tzu said he had just three things to teach:
Simplicity, patience and kindness.
He said these three are your greatest treasures.
It seems they would lead to peacefulness.

"Simplicity and repose are the qualities that measure
The true value of any work of art."
So says Frank Lloyd Wright, an architect of renown.
He believed it with all his heart.

Prosperity

Prosperity is one of those concepts which requires
It's opposite in order to fully understand
The meaning, with all of its nuances and elements.
So bear with me as I further expand.

The opposite, of course, is adversity – you know –
That part we experience that tests our courage.
Without the need to overcome adversity,
Prosperity would not be so sweet a package.

If we had no winter, spring would not be as pleasant.
(How would we know when it arrived?)
Adversity has the effect of eliciting talents
To overcome one's condition and thrive.

"A man is insensible to the relish of prosperity,"
So states Sa'di, a Persian poet of old.
He finished the thought: " ...till he has tasted adversity."
(This is thirteenth century wisdom to behold.)

SOLITUDE

Guard well your spare moments; they're like uncut diamonds.
Discard them and their value will never be known.
Instead, you must improve them and value them highly.
For a useful life they become the brightest gems you own.

Montaigne said it best, "The greatest thing in the world
Is to know how to belong to oneself." Total.
The fear of finding one's self alone can be so great
That most people don't find themselves at all.

In order to be open to the creative muses
You must constructively use your times of solitude.
It is within your power to retire into yourself
Whenever you choose to seek quietude.

In solitude your mind can focus inwardly,
Organizing its processes away from distractions.
You create an internal state of resonance
Before entering again in your many interactions.

It's said that solitude is strength, and I can believe it.
Depending on presence of a crowd is weakness.
Solitude is where you discover you're not alone.
It's the house of peace. You always have access.

Solitude is the soul in which genius is planted,
Where creativity grows and where legends bloom.
Make friends with yourself. You'll never be alone.
To explore all your options you have ample elbow room.

David James Duncan, in his novel *The River Why*,
Said, "Solitude was raw material... older than men...
And it was merciless — for it let a man become
Precisely what he alone made of himself." Amen.

RELATIONSHIPS

Suppose a movie was made of your life,
And all the relationships you have had.
And when it was shown on the big wide screen,
Would you be happy or sad?

We seem to choose people to be in our lives
So that we can learn and grow.
Sometimes it doesn't turn out as we'd hoped,
But at least we 'gave it a go.'

For me, I know that there have been
Many, many mistakes on my part.
I am in hope the errors were innocent,
And that I escaped with a pure heart.

I read this thought once, and it seems to be true:
"If measuring your relationship is a concern –
You can tell how much you are giving it
By how much you get in return."

It's good to be a friend, and to be trusted to grow –
And learn and change along the way.
How will your friends who are closest to you
Write your obituary some day?

CHARITY

Simple acts of kindness, such as charitable acts...
Or expressing gratitude for gifts received
Have a positive effect on our long-term needs.
This statement, in fact, is easily believed.

"Where there is charity and wisdom," said St. Francis,
"There is neither fear nor ignorance..." present.
Every good act is charity, and true wealth
Is the good one does for others with good intent.

Bob Hope said it well, on the subject of charity:
(He was a man who lived large and was not very subtle.)
"If you haven't got any charity in your heart
You have the {very} worst kind of heart trouble."

Charity does not always come in the form
Of money from people who have the means.
Give a gift of friendship to overwhelm the loneliness
That grips others' lives, and change their routines.

ADVENT TIME

Advent time is a happy time
To celebrate the love...
Love of self, and love of others,
And love from Heaven above.

The little gifts are tokens, my dears –
Tokens of my esteem.
In some small way, they're here to say
"I love you," and I deem
You're two of the greatest gifts to me.
You're special in every way.
If Christmas is a celebration of love,
Then with you, Christmas is every day!

SHINE YOUR LIGHT

If you are comparing yourself to others,
There's no chance for being the best you can be.
You must discover your own personal gifts,
And let them shine for all to see.

The best way to do that is to be your own self.
What you are and what you believe
Will come shining through so brightly, it will...
In every part of your life, you'll achieve.

Whatever is going on around you can be
Overcome by the belief that resides in you.
The belief in your light that lives inside
Will give you the courage to continue.

The more you adhere to the truth as you know it,
The brighter you will shine your light.
You do not need to outshine your neighbor;
You need only to shine with all your might.

As you let your own light shine around others
You are giving permission for them to do the same.
Be a source of strength and also of courage.
Radiate love... it's your perpetual flame.

THE RIPPLE EFFECT

Do you want to have a positive effect,
Or remain forever neutral?
In order to be an influence to anyone,
I hereby make this proposal:
Ground yourself, put your life in order
So that your behavior is wholesome.
It will earn you respect and credibility,
And show others a way to overcome.

Your behavior influences others through
An effect that is known as 'ripple.'
It works because everyone is touched
By everyone else in the circle.

If your life works, your family is influenced.
Going forward, the community is perfected...
Community to state, and then to nation...
The nation to the world... all affected.

Remember that all the positive begins,
By your influence, with you.
It ripples outward and knows no limits.
(The negative is also true.)

OPPORTUNITY

Change in one's life brings opportunity
To overcome crisis, take a new direction…
To do things you thought you couldn't do before…
To begin again, with additional circumspection.

The ladder of success, it is said, is best climbed
By stepping on the rungs of opportunity.
The secret is to be ready when opportunities arise
And acting on them with great impunity.

When a great moment knocks on the door of your life
It's often no louder than the beating of your heart.
It's very easy to miss the chance…
So listen closely, be ready and be smart.

A pessimist sees difficulty in every opportunity…
An optimist, opportunity in each difficulty.
Be an optimist, be prepared, and seize the chance
To change things for the better with faculty.

"Opportunity is missed by most people because
It is dressed in overalls and looks like work."
Thomas Edison is credited with the above quote.
With his track record, his labors he did not shirk.

Men make history! It's not the other way around.
Society stands still without a strong leader.
Progress occurs when opportunities are seized
To change things for the better with no impeder.

Your big opportunity may be right where you are.
Don't get too comfortable with who you are now,
Because you might miss the opportunity to become
Who you want to be, dreams fulfilled, somehow.

DOING

If you want to understand what a watermelon is
Take a watermelon, and get a knife –
Then cut it and put a slice in your mouth –
That is your experience – your life.

And again, not mere talk about water, the well,
Or the sight of a spring with bubbling action,
But an actual mouthful to quench your thirst
And give you complete satisfaction.

The doing, the experiencing, is what gives meaning;
It's the most direct path to belief.
After reading and imagining and discussing for years,
Jump right in, take action for relief!

A CLOSING THOUGHT

POETRY

It's the revelation
Of a sensation
That the poet
(Wouldn't you know it)
Believes to be
Felt only interiorly
And personal to
The writer who
... **writes it.**

It's the interpretation
Of a sensation
That was fueled by
A poet's sigh
And believed to be
Shared mutually
And personal to
The lucky one who
... **reads it.**

About the author

Kathryn Carole Ellison is a former newspaper columnist
and journalist and, of course, a poet.

She lives near her children and stepchildren and their families in the
Pacific Northwest, and spends winters in the sunshine of Arizona.

You might find her on the golf course with friends, river rafting, traveling
the world, writing poems... or enjoying the Opera and the Symphony.

Late bloomer

Our culture honors youth with all
It's unbridled effervescence.
We older ones sit back and nod
As if in acquiescence.

And when our confidence really gels
In early convalescence...
"We can't be getting old!" we cry,
"We're still struggling with adolescence!"

Acknowledgments

I have many people to thank...

First of all, my amazing children—Jon and Nicole LaFollette—for inspiring the writing of these poems in the first place. And for encouraging me to continue my writing, even though their wisdom and compassion surpass mine... and to my dear daughter-in-law and friend, Eva LaFollette, whose encouragement and interest are so appreciated.

My wonderful stepchildren, Debbie and John Bacon, Jeff and Sandy Ellison, and Tom and Sue Ellison who, with their children and grandchildren, continue to be a major part of my life; and are loved deeply by me. These poems are for you, too.

My good friends who have received a poem or two of mine in their Christmas cards these many years, for complimenting me on the messages in my poems. Your encouragement kept me writing and gave me the courage to publish.

To Kim Kiyosaki who introduced me to the right person to get the publishing process under way... Mona Gambetta with Brisance Books Group. I marvel at her experience and know-how to make these books happen.

To Amy Anderson, Sonya Kopetz, Kerri Kazarba Schneider, and Ingrid Pape-Sheldon, my very creative public relations team of experts, who have carried my story to the world.

And finally, to John B. Laughlin, a fellow traveler in life, who encourages me every day in the writing and publishing process. John, I love having you in my cheering section.

BOOKS OF LOVE
by Kathryn Carole Ellison

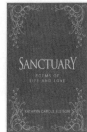